RIDDLES FOR KIDS

The Book with 450 Puzzles, including Riddles and Quizzes to entertain your child and stimulate interest in an educational way.

Rossana Vittori

Copyright © 2023 – Rossana Vittori

All rights reserved.

This document is intended to provide accurate and reliable information on the topic and issue discussed. The publication is sold with the understanding that the publisher is not required to provide accounting services, officially authorized or otherwise qualified. If advice, legal or professional, is required, an individual practiced in the profession should be consulted. It is not legal in any way to reproduce, duplicate, or transmit any part of this document in electronic or paper format. The recording of this publication is strictly prohibited, and the storage of this document is not allowed without the written permission of the publisher. All rights reserved.

The information provided in this document is stated to be truthful and consistent, as any liability, in terms of negligence or otherwise, from any use or misuse of any policy, process, or direction contained within is the sole and absolute responsibility of the intended reader. In no event will any legal liability or blame be taken against the publisher for any reparation, damage, or monetary loss due to the information herein, directly or indirectly.

The information contained herein is provided for informational purposes only and is universal. The presentation of the information is without contract or any type of guarantee. The trademarks used within this book are for clarification purposes only and are the property of their respective owners, not affiliated with this document.

SUMMARY

INTRODUCTION 6

    RIDDLES 6

    OUR MISSION 19

    SMALL GLOSSARY 22

SIMPLE RIDDLES (1-90) 26

    SIMPLE RIDDLE SOLUTIONS 38

INTERMEDIATE RIDDLES (1-96) 44

    INTERMEDIATE RIDDLE SOLUTIONS 55

MASTER RIDDLES (1-95) 61

    MASTER RIDDLE SOLUTIONS 73

THE CHARM OF QUIZZES 79

GENERAL KNOWLEDGE QUIZZES 83

    GENERAL KNOWLEDGE QUIZ SOLUTIONS 89

FILM & CARTOON QUIZZES 92

    FILM & CARTOON QUIZ SOLUTIONS 99

VARIOUS SPORTS QUIZZES 102
Various sports quiz solutions 109

CONCLUSIONS 112
DEEP DIVE: CHILDREN AND LATERAL THINKING 112
DEEP DIVE: HUMOROUS RIDDLES 118
SOLUTIONS 121
DEEP DIVE: THE CHARADE 123

IN CONCLUSION 125

INTRODUCTION

RIDDLES

What they are: As a classic definition, a riddle is a game consisting of written text, generally in the form of an epigram. Usually, it is defined as a composition that is distinguished by its brevity and incisiveness. Each game has a purpose, and in this case, it is to guess the object hidden behind the verses, keeping in mind that the composition itself has a double meaning. It presents a "real" one behind a more immediate, "apparent" one.

Riddles differ from enigmas in their greater brevity and simplicity, being lighter, and having another peculiarity: they do not actually have a defined solution, to suggest with numerical diagrams, like a rebus. A synonym of the word to be guessed may also be correct, instead of the one we originally thought of.

In terms of structure, the game includes the name ("Riddle"), a "title" (which refers to the apparent meaning), and a "development" (which seems to continue to refer to the apparent meaning but actually conceals the real one). The title, in our riddles, is not present, if not in a minimal part, also because it is usually used to mislead and divert, thus increasing the level of difficulty, while the standard of this book's proposal is intriguing but aimed at a children and teenagers audience, not at adults or experienced enigmatists.

Some riddles are real rhyming nursery rhymes (four lines: AABB, ABAB, ABBA crossed rhyme), others similar to "jokes," significantly more concise, others boast a metrical structure, quatrains, or sextets of hendecasyllables. It should be emphasized that the need to harmonize the elegance of the composition (the "musicality") and the strength of the enigmatic discovery generally leads to compromises and the overcoming of too rigid schemes: they can, therefore, present assonances or a single rhyme.

To be used as "useful entertainment," they must meet certain specific characteristics. The solutions must not be excessively "specialized": the riddle must describe common objects or situations, easily recognizable by the widest range of solvers. It is not advisable to suggest, as answers, overly defined and complex situations, but also overly abstract ones, and it is also necessary to avoid relying exclusively on humor to create nonsensical answers, cute but too difficult to guess. There is also the opposite problem, of course: the riddle must not be too descriptive. In this case, the error would be in the text, while in the previous case, it concerned the solution.

What they are for: For children and teenagers, riddles are something that helps stimulate independent thinking and creativity. They create interactions and help socialize "in real-time." They also offer the opportunity to learn, not only for the knowledge but also for the possibility of reflecting on various aspects of nature and the animal world. And, of course, they can be solved and then reformulated, feeding an oral heritage in times otherwise dominated by writing and technology. They are a fun way to spend time and have fun trying to refine everyone's logical and investigative skills, in short, they are real puzzles to be solved in the company, which make both adults and children spend quality time.

They can enliven a car trip while on vacation, entertain everyone at a birthday party, or be included, along with other ideas, in a fun outdoor treasure hunt.

Children's creativity is their first tool for learning and understanding, and so inventing stories together with them, playing with riddles, and inventing lullabies and nursery rhymes will help them develop cognitive faculties.

Riddles require cognitive skills, forcing a pleasant reasoning process and distracting children by involving them in a game that takes them away from the technology they sometimes seem to be too accustomed to. In addition to being entertaining, riddles are very effective in training children's attention span and helping their concentration, just like books.

The most famous riddle of antiquity: in Greek mythology, it is said that the Sphinx, a creature with a woman's face, a lion's body, and bird wings, posed a riddle to passersby at the entrance of the city of Thebes. Those who did not answer were subject to strangulation or being devoured (sources differ on the type of punishment). The proposed riddle is still popular today, but few can connect it to this ancient myth. The Sphinx, sent by Hera and crouching on Mount Phicium, asks:

"Who, despite having only one voice, transforms into a quadruped, a tripod, or a biped?". In a similar version, reported in Greek by Diodorus Siculus: "Who is simultaneously a biped, a tripod, and a quadruped?". Oedipus, in the myth, correctly answered "Man", causing the Sphinx's suicide as it threw itself from the Acropolis.

The reference is to the different stages of life, with crawling on all fours in infancy followed by the upright posture of maturity, and finally, the elderly person walking and relying on a cane for support.

The riddles of "The Lord of the Rings": In J.R.R. Tolkien's famous book, the "battle" of riddles between the hobbit Bilbo Baggins and the creature Gollum is described (and then adapted in the film version). In this case, too, the wordplay remains relevant, even though the work dates back to the first half of the twentieth century. Some examples:

It has invisible roots, it stands higher than trees, it goes up among the clouds, but it will never grow (solution: the mountain)

Thirty white horses on a red hill, they beat and bite, but none has moved (solution: teeth)

It has no voice, yet it makes cries, it has no wings, yet it flies, it has no teeth, yet it bites, it has no mouth, yet it makes sounds (solution: the wind)

You can't see it nor hear it, you can't smell it nor detect it. It lies beneath the hills, behind the stars, and fills all empty spaces and cells. It comes first and goes last, it brings life and laughter to an end (solution: darkness)

Without a lid, key, or hinge, a chest hides a golden sphere (solution: the egg)

It lives without breathing, it seems as cold as death, it drinks but is never thirsty, it doesn't jingle when armored (solution: the fish)

Bilbo Baggins will win the contest by asking a direct question that has none of the typical characteristics of riddles, namely, "What do I have in my pocket?" An irregularity that, in the narrative, will save his life.

All types of riddles: Riddles are not only divided by the level of difficulty but also by the target audience, the fixed "theme," or the form.

Mathematical Riddles: Not very present in this text due to a specific choice, they are halfway between the classic riddle and the enigmatic puzzle in the strict sense. Sometimes they are accompanied by explanatory figures or drawings. They are also defined as a mix between a game and a school lesson, a fun way to review formulas and concepts. We propose some examples (with solutions) in order of difficulty:

A brick weighs 1kg plus half a brick: how much does it weigh? (a brick = half a brick + half a brick; a brick = half a brick + 1 kg; half a brick = 1 kg; a brick = 2 kg)

There is a tree with two branches. On both branches, some birds are perched. Guess how many birds are on the top branch and the bottom branch, knowing that: a) if one of the birds goes down, those below become double the number of those above; b) if one of the birds goes up, they become equal. (There are 5 birds above, 7 below)

An old 45 rpm record is engraved in the area between the diameters of 17 and 11 cm, and it takes 2 minutes and 30 seconds to listen to it. How long is the path the stylus travels from the beginning to the end of the record? (3 cm. During the record playback, the stylus, regardless of the speed of the record and the listening time, moves - approximately - along the radius towards the center of the record. The useful diameter is 6 cm, so the useful radius is exactly half)

Logical Riddles: A riddle of this type is usually posed in the form of a question that can be answered through reasoning or intuition, not due to specific knowledge of the proposed subjects. The most common formula is to present the solver with a paradoxical situation and ask how it is possible at the same time. The first impression for the player is that the problem is insoluble and there is no answer. To find it, they will have to change their perspective of reasoning, thus admitting that they were wrong in their initial approach. This is an aspect that is sometimes defined as "philosophical," and indeed a very common subcategory of this type of riddle is called "Aristotelian": these are games where the information is presented incompletely, and the solver can venture into some clarifying questions, naturally with a blocked response (yes/no). The other category is called "complete initial information," and in that case, you can immediately try to solve it. Some examples:

(paradoxical logical with complete information)

A man has two girlfriends, one in the Bronx and one in Brooklyn. Every day he goes to visit one of them. However, not knowing which one to choose, he goes to the subway station and takes the first train heading to either of the two destinations. Knowing that:

- a train to the Bronx passes (and stops at the station) every hour;
- a train to Brooklyn passes (and stops at the station) every hour;
- the trains' stop at the station is of equal duration;
- Bronx and Brooklyn, compared to the station, are in opposite directions (no train stops at both stations);
- the man enters the station whenever it happens, without any particular regularity;
- the trains pass through the same platform (the man actually takes the first of the two that passes through the station)

- explain why the man goes to his girlfriend in Brooklyn more than 90% of the days.

- Solution: The two trains pass once every hour, but the train to the Bronx passes a few minutes after the one to Brooklyn (precisely 6 minutes later). For example, the train to Brooklyn may pass at 4:30 pm and the one to the Bronx at 4:36 pm, and so on for the other hours. If the man arrives in those six minutes (with a 10% chance in an hour), he will go to the Bronx. If instead, he arrives during the other 54 minutes (with a 90% chance), he will wait for the train to Brooklyn.

- (Aristotelian logic with partial information)

- The situation: Juliet and Romeo are dead on the floor. There is water and broken glass on the ground. The window is open. Explain how the two died.

- Solution: The key to the riddle is that they are fish. Juliet and Romeo were in their glass bowl, near a window, when a gust of wind suddenly blew it wide open, hitting the bowl hard enough to knock it to the ground, breaking it (hence the explanation for the shards of glass and water on the floor) and causing the fish to die from lack of water.

Word Games: Riddles of this type are said to be "apparently" logical, revealing a humorous nature in reality. They are based on word games, precisely, or real traps, and therefore appear strongly "misleading" to those who venture into their solution. An example:

(trap)

A breeder has 40 sheep. On Monday, a fire kills half of them. On Tuesday, a fifth of the sheep manages to escape. On Wednesday, the breeder buys ten new animals. How many cows does he own in the end?

Solution: Who ever mentioned cows?

OUR MISSION

It's no secret that, nowadays, children spend much of their free time playing with technological devices or immersed in the world of social networks. Adults and children alike go through their days almost mechanically, without emotional involvement, without real socialization, staring at a screen and self-isolating. Entertainment with modern electronic devices is not inherently bad; it's the way we use them that makes something virtuous or harmful. Often, there are no genuinely creative and stimulating alternatives, so dependence on devices and social media becomes a kind of "escape."

Imagine a family car trip. The father watches the road and listens to his favorite music using the car radio's Bluetooth system. The mother scrolls through Facebook in the passenger seat. In the back, the daughter wears headphones to listen to her own music downloaded on her phone while scrolling through Instagram. The son, also wearing headphones, plays a Formula 1 GP simulation or a management game on his phone. This situation is typical nowadays. How much more productive, socializing, and interactive it would be if the father proposed a riddle to the children, and they helped each other with the answer, exulting proudly in the case of a correct solution. And how much more effective it would be if the children themselves proposed a game from the back seat, laughing at their parents' disjointed answers or admiring the acuity of whoever was ready to respond correctly.

This is a trivial example of what inspires this book: rediscovering human relationships and simple, genuine fun.

The same goes for quizzes. Imagine a Christmas table laden with food. Lunch has just ended, and relatives start challenging each other with cross-answer quizzes. Whoever answers correctly proposes the next one and chooses the topic, and so on. Cinema, Sports,

Music, History, Geography, Sciences. A way to savor true conviviality and strengthen relationships, deepen knowledge and empathy, instead of just eating together and immediately taking pictures of the dishes, posting "stories" on Instagram or TikTok, and "isolating" in company.

Children have an extraordinary and primordial capacity for intuition and imagination. It's important to help them not to become flat, to stimulate their natural curiosity about the world around them. Imagination is a real wealth for the mind, the only antidote to apathy. It's not just an attitude to make the best use of free time, but a genuine characteristic of the individual. Creativity is a gift to cultivate also because it allows us to see reality through less rigid patterns and not mediated by adult preconceptions. In the early years of education and teaching, it's important to involve children with music, poetry, stories, and, yes, even nursery rhymes and riddles.

The ability to ponder, converse, and draw reasoned conclusions based on our experiences is what truly makes us human. It allows us to communicate, build, and progress beyond the level or stage reached by our civilization.

SMALL GLOSSARY

Bluetooth: Bluetooth is a technical-industrial standard for wireless personal data transmission. It provides a standard, affordable, and secure method for exchanging information between different devices.

Creativity: a term that refers to the cognitive ability of the mind to invent or create, and, at the same time, to think outside the box or explore unknown paths.

Device: a noun in computer language that means "electronic device." Adding the adjective Mobile refers to all those electronic devices that are fully usable following the user's mobility, such as cell phones, PDAs, smartphones, tablets, notebooks, MP3 players, GPS receivers, etc.

Enigmatology: the art of composing and solving enigmatic puzzles, that is, games that hide a solution concealed within the author according to the specific criteria of each type.

Facebook: a community, blog, chat, forum, instant messaging service, email service, and more, as well as a powerful advertising and communication tool. Originally created as a system for finding classmates or former colleagues online and exchanging memories and greetings.

Nursery rhymes: a song or rhythmic composition (sometimes in the form of dialogue), generally in short assonant or rhymed meters, with a fast rhythm, made up of phrases connected by merely verbal links, recited or sung by children in their games, or by adults to entertain, calm, or put children to sleep.

Riddles: a short popular enigma, generally in easy and rhymed verses, sometimes introduced by a fixed formula, which humorously and ambiguously describes the qualities or characteristics of the person, animal, concrete or abstract thing that must be guessed.

Instagram: Instagram is an American social networking service that allows users to take photos, apply filters, and share them online.

Quiz: a prepared question or problem posed to test the cultural, general or specific preparation, or memory, of candidates, contestants, and the like, or as a personality analysis test. The term is mainly used to indicate the questions that are an element of many games and prize competitions in newspapers, magazines, radio, and television.

Scroll: From the English "scroll," it refers to the action of scrolling up or down along a page on a mobile device or computer screen using a mouse wheel or touchpad.

Social Network: over the years, the term has evolved from referring to a group of people actually linked by social relationships and studied by sociology, to virtual meeting points offered to internet users to exchange videos, messages, chat, get information, share photos, and more. All managed through applications designed for mobile devices, thus staying connected to the web even away from home PCs.

Stories: Instagram Stories are texts, photos, and short videos (lasting up to 15 seconds) that can be added to a dedicated section of one's Instagram profile, where they remain visible for 24 hours.

TikTok: also known as Douyin in China, is a Chinese social network launched in September 2016, initially under the name musical.ly. Through the app, users can create short music clips of variable duration (up to 15 or up to 60 seconds) and optionally change playback speed, add filters, and special effects to their videos.

SIMPLE RIDDLES
(1-90)

1 - I live in ponds, I am an animal. At night, I sing. Four legs, but no tail. What am I?

2 - Turn us on our backs, open us on our bellies, and thanks to us, you'll become wiser! What are we?

3 - Guess, riddle. I am close to a knife. When you're hungry, you grab me quickly, you got it, I am a ....

4 - I am in the meadow and children like me, I am dressed in polka dots, I am round and so beautiful, everyone calls me ....

5 - My name is Fido. I live on a farm with four dogs: Nembo, Jack, Ugo, Speedy. What is the name of the fifth dog?

6 - I live wild in the forest, I have ears bigger than my head, I have a long and heavy nose, here I am, I am ....

7 - Betta's mother has three daughters. One is named Sara. One is named Camilla. What is the name of the third daughter?

8 - I can be of many colors, and I am bigger when I am full. If you don't tie me, it's trouble, I fly so far away that you can't even see me. What am I?

9 - I am at the station to carry people, you can travel in a flash because I am called the ...

10 - For the fragrant hair, I am remembered by everyone, I sting kings and queens too, be careful of my thorns, I am a gift for the bride, and they call me the....

11 - I am tiny, chubby, sweet, and brownish, I am a mountain breed and queen in the autumn, I am the children's delight, yes, my name is...

12 - I am small and flying, and I have a buzzing sound, but if I want, I can enter a castle to eat. Who am I?

13 - I never take off my pajamas, yet I don't sleep on a bed...I have a tail and a mane, but I am not a horse. What am I?

14 - What happens if you throw a white hat into the Black Sea?

15 - Without doing anything, I make you shiver, especially in winter you can meet me. Who am I?

16 - I am long and narrow like a snake, but instead of biting, I am useful to people. What am I?

17 - I have wings, but I cannot fly, I spend all day pecking. Who am I?

18 - I am neither a pen nor a pencil, I can write but I strain your fingers.

19 - Half mouse and half bird, I sleep upside down and my name is....

20 - Sometimes they are boring, and you'd rather play, but if you want to do well in school, you must finish them. What are they?

21 - Round like a ball, transparent like glass, I let myself be carried by the wind, then I burst, never going back. What am I?

22 - I move high up on a tower, I make so much noise that it can be heard in the village and marks the passing of the hours. What am I?

23 - I swim in the sea, but I also like to jump...people say I am intelligent. Who am I?

24 - It cannot be seen or touched... it always comes out of the mouth. What is it?

25 - The hotter I am, the fresher I am, what a grotesque phenomenon. What am I?

26 - Delivers postcards, bills, and little letters, by car or foot you know me, I am.......

27 - They sure have class, brunettes, blondes, tall or short, they don't work in the

countryside, but always beside the blackboard. Who are they?

28 - Many kilometers in just a few hours, I control a great engine, to travel in debt, only with me can you fly. Who am I?

29 - Stops the driver, checks who comes, so that everyone behaves well; helps those in difficulty, and this is their skill. Who is it?

30 - If I'm good, I shine like the sky, a stage or a film is my moment. I don't like collecting tomatoes, but only applause and honors. Who am I?

31 - If you don't speak first, I am nothing... who am I?

32 - They don't have hands... but they make noise every hour. What are we talking about?

33 - What has four legs... but can't walk?

34 - I can pass through glass without breaking it... what am I?

35 - It enters only if you turn its head. What is it?

36- I am just like you, I follow you all day long, but when darkness comes, I quickly hide. What am I?

37 - It cannot be seen in the sky... an angel has one... in paradise there are two, and throughout the universe... none can be found. What is it?

38 - With the things it does, it has importance, and if it's put in a box, it doesn't mean it's foolish. The....

39 - It always falls from the clouds. What is it?

40 - They are two sisters who run and watch each other but never touch. What are they?

41 - What is it that the larger it is, the lighter it is?

42 - If I get scared, I can hurt you, but I try not to because stinging kills me. Who am I?

43 - Even if it doesn't wear makeup, it's always attractive... what is it?

44 - What contains sugar but is not sweet at all?

45 - In the water, they are called fish, but in the mountains, they are alpine. We are talking about....

46 - What is it that the more you look at it... the less you see?

47 - I live in the woods, I am wider than long, I am under the hat, and I am a...

48 - What can you beat by playing, even when you don't win anything?

49 - It is in rain and frost, but it is missing in dew. What is it?

50 - I am born white, fresh, and beautiful with a mischievous face, I have a great fear of the sun, it destroys me in a few hours. What am I?

51 - It has two wings and doesn't fly slowly; it is featherless and is an...

52 - It gets lit only once. What is it?

53 - They are four sisters who cannot be seen, and when one comes, the other goes away. Who are they?

54 - Who undresses when it's cold?

55 - One always overtakes on the right, the other always on the left, and when they cross, it's trouble. Who are they?

56 - With you, I take away the cold, with you, I cook, but it's better if you don't stay too close to me. Who am I talking about?

57 - In winter it often drips, and not just from one side, when it itches you can blow it, but without a mirror, you can't observe it. What is it?

58 - I scratch my ears with my nose, and I also use it to eat if necessary. Who am I?

59 - If you throw it, it runs and jumps, it often excites soccer players. What is it?

60 - Guess, guess what, you know, I drive a beautiful boat, when I want to change direction, it's quite simple, I am the...

61 - I can't stand up, nor straight, if you break me, I am... fried. What am I?

62 - It has a ruby-red crown, but it eats grains and some seeds. It has a pair of wings but can't fly, who knows who it is... can you guess?

63 - On the tower from morning to evening, there is an old figure, always wiggling a tooth to call all the people... no, it's not something strange, it's just a...

64 - You rub me every morning, and the more you rub me, the smaller I become. Who am I?

65 - We are small and greenish, all round, little brothers, we stay inside pods and they call us...

66 - They stay together in the red stable, thirty beautiful white horses, and they are never tired, all standing at attention, you got it, we are...

67 - Red and small, I stay in the damp cage, hopping here and there, who knows my name?

68 - I can be white and I can be red, if you drink too much of me, you'll fall into a ditch. Be careful not to overdo it, because my dear, I will make you drunk. What am I?

69 - I am agile and moustached, the terror of every bird. I hunt mice, only the dog threatens me. Who am I?

70 - In the nativity scene, I am the protagonist, you recognize me at first sight, I blow and warm the little baby, I am not the ox but...

71 - You can find me in the fireplace, with a single blow you make me fly. Who am I?

72 - As soon as I dive into the sea, I can only sink. I am heavy, in fact, and I can't swim. Who am I?

73 - I fill children's hearts, I can be of various colors. If you let go of my string, I can finally fly. Who am I?

74 - I am not an apple, nor a pear, but my body is still sphere-shaped. I am not an orange, nor a melon, until you peel me, I am all orange. Who am I?

75 - In the woods in the summer, we are hidden on small plants, we are fresh and fragrant, we are the tasty...

76 - I have whiskers and a keen sense of smell, I can smell a mouse, I go crazy with wool, make way, I am the...

77 - At first sight... it's ugly, it smells a lot, more than anything, if you touch it, it's also hairy, then you eat it... and it's tasty. What is it?

78 - At most, I can be for milk, but never for coffee

79 - You scratch it even if it doesn't itch. What is it?

80 - Who is it that, if you're not the first to speak, won't respond to you?

81 - During the day, sometimes, I am empty, at night I am often full. If the weather is bad, I have a sloping roof. What am I?

82 - I am tall and with a long beard, if you use me I wear out. I can help with household chores, but it is on me that witches manage to fly. What am I?

83 - I live on the roof, and I never go to bed. Night and day I smoke, but I emit a good smell. Who am I?

84 - What is it that is multicolored and colorful, and after the rain shows its splendor?

85 - I am immobile at intersections, I constantly change color. With green, I like to let you pass, but with red, you have to stop. What am I?

86 - I am not raw, but always well-cooked. You can dip me in milk, I am a...

87 - I am often beautiful, and always fragrant, my destiny is to be born in the meadow. Thin or large, of any color, I fill gardens and they call me...

88 - It arrives between winds and fright, it is angry and ominous, here is the...

89 - What is it that no one can see, but everyone feels coming?

90 - I am in the field all day, and I have no birds around. Even though I am dressed as a farmer, I don't move a finger all day. Who am I?

Simple Riddle Solutions

1 - Frog

2 - Books

3 - Fork

4 - Ladybug

5 - Fido

6 - Elephant

7 - Betta

8 - Balloon

9 - Train

10 - Rose

11 - The chestnut

12 - Fly

13 - Zebra

14 - It gets wet

15 - Cold

16 - Rope

17 - Chicken

18 - Chalk

19 - Bat

20 - Homework

21 - Soap bubble

22 - Bell

23 - Dolphin

24 - Word

25 - Bread

26 - Mailman

27 - Teacher

28 - Pilot

29 - Police officer

30 - Actor

31 - Echo

32 - Bells

33 - Table

34 - Light

35 - Screw

36 - Shadow

37 - The letter "A"

38 - Brain

39 - Rain

40 - The banks of a river

41 - A hole

42 - Bee

43 - Magnet

44 - Sugar bowl

45 - Stars

46 - Sun

47 - Mushroom

48 - Boredom

49 - The letter "R"

50 - Snowman

51 - Airplane

52 - Match

53 - Seasons

54 - Tree

55 - Feet

56 - Fire

57 - Nose

58 - Elephant

59 - Ball

60 - Rudder

61 - Egg

62 - Chicken

63 - Bell

64 - Soap bar

65 - Peas

66 - Teeth

67 - Tongue

68 - Wine

69 - Cat

70 - Donkey

71 - Ashes

72 - Anchor

73 - Balloon

74 - Mandarin

75 - Strawberries

76 - Cat

77 - Pig

78 - Cow

79 - Parmesan cheese

80 - Echo

81 - House

82 - Broom

83 - Chimney

84 - Rainbow

85 - Traffic light

86 - Cookie

87 - Flower

88 - Storm

89 - Voice

90 – Scarecrow

INTERMEDIATE RIDDLES (1-96)

1 - What is full of holes, but doesn't let water through?

2 - It becomes damp when it dries.

3 - What is easy to enter, but hard to exit?

4 - It has a neck ... but not a head. What is it?

5 - What has legs... but doesn't walk?

6 - Children unwrap it ... yet everyone loves to eat it. What is it?

7 - What needs to be broken before you can use it?

8 - It knows many things, even if it cannot speak. Those who want to learn ... can consult it. What is it?

9 - I am tall when I am young, short when I am old. What am I?

10 - You enter a cold room that contains: a candle, a fireplace, a match, a kerosene lamp. What do you light first?

11 - Two heads, four eyes, six legs... and a tail. What is it?

12 - It travels around the world, but stays in one place. What is it?

13 - Students look at me once a day; some keep one a secret.

14 - I have no life, but I can die. What am I?

15 - It has a bed but doesn't sleep. It runs but doesn't walk. What are we talking about?

16 - Everyone has it; no one can lose it. What is it?

17 - Three men are on a boat. The boat capsizes. Only two get their hair wet. Why?

18 - I have a thumb and four other fingers, but I have no life. What am I?

19 - What has only one eye, but cannot see?

20 - If you're in a race and overtake the person in second place, what position are you in?

21 - When I arrive, damage comes, I break cars, tear clothes. I'm cold to the touch, I accumulate below, but in no time you won't see me anymore.

22 - I don't speak, I don't hear, but I tell the truth. Who am I?

23 - I don't have wings, but I can fly... I don't have eyes, but I can cry. What am I?

24 - If you give me water, I will die. What am I?

25 - I'm always still, I never move, but if I smoke and grumble, trouble comes. What am I?

26 - It's tied but innocent, very much liked by many people.

27 - Which bird... can lift a weight?

28 - What was the first planet discovered by man?

29 - It's black when it's clean, white when it's dirty. What is it?

30 - Who married many women but never got married?

31 - What do you have in December that you don't have in any other month?

32 - They fill me with food, but I can't eat anything. What am I?

33 - Everyone can open it, but no one can close it again. What is it?

34 - You will never eat me, but you will buy me to eat, and when you eat, I will be there. Who am I?

35 - They come out at night without being invited, disappear during the day without being stolen. Who are they?

36 - I have only one letter... but I start with E and end with E. What am I?

37 - It's a table... but it doesn't have legs. What is it?

38 - I exist only when there is light... but with direct light, I no longer exist. What am I?

39 - We open them in the morning when we wake up. What are they?

40 - You get it when it's cold. You can pass it, but you can't throw it away. What is it?

41 - It can only be done with closed eyes. What is it?

42 - I come to you to remove the troubles. Who am I?

43 - Students look at me once a day, some keep me a secret. Who am I?

44 - What is it that we throw away, and then eat?

45 - I have a needle but can't sew, however, I can tell you the direction. What am I?

46 - I have married many people, but no one has ever married me. Who am I?

47 - I have brains and liver for sale. Who am I?

48 - When they arrive, everyone leaves. What are they?

49 - I cross the meadow without walking on it. What am I?

50 - We are dancers, but if we oscillate, we fall, and not only in children. What are we?

51 - What is it that only enters if you turn its head?

52 - In the morning they leave me, but in the evening, they always return to me. What are they?

53 - What has six faces, and one always looks at the ground?

54 - What can be lengthened, but not shortened?

55 - What has a head but no body?

56 - It whistles without a mouth, lashes you but doesn't touch you, runs without feet, passes and you don't see it. What is it?

57 - I am a battlefield with black and white soldiers, when one goes crazy, my war is already over.

58 - I stand on wheat and over a ditch, I don't burn but wear fire. Who am I?

59 - If I am in love, I sing all night long; I jump among flowers and grass, and for children, catching me is a boast. Who am I?

60 - They arrive, and everyone leaves. What are we talking about?

61 - I write... and I write, but I can't read what I write. Who am I?

62 - I have teeth, but I don't bite... I pass by, and everyone takes off their hat. Who am I?

63 - It's the only place where you'll find Thursday before Wednesday. What are we talking about?

64 - What has holes everywhere but holds water?

65 - When you stand up, they lie down, but when you lie down... they stand up. What are they?

66 - I can be made of paper or metal, I pass from hand to hand, and everyone is crazy about me. I am...

67 - You can find me in clothes, sometimes hidden, sometimes evident. I serve to warm hands or put things away, but often contain nothing. What am I?

68 - In the summer, you can hear me singing, they say I don't feel like doing anything; in fairy tales, I meet a friend, I am... and she is the ant.

69 - If you slice an onion, they won't be late to arrive. They can be salty or sentimental, in front of great pain, you won't be able to hold them back. What are they?

70 - In grains and divided by colors, I am an important food and they call me...

71 - What can jump the floors of a building, but not obstacles?

72 - I have to do with fishing and the circus: the more broken I am, the fewer holes I have. What am I?

73 - Green it is born, red it dies, the taste is delicious. Which vegetable are we talking about?

74 - What crosses a meadow while standing still?

75 - I accompany myself, on the table, with the knife. When the food comes, you take me quickly; I indeed serve you to eat, I am the...

76 - When it's daytime, it rises silently... but eventually wakes everyone up. What is it?

77 - We are twenty-four, we arrive every day, and every day, one at a time, we leave. What are we?

78 - What is greeted only when raised?

79 - It has horns and climbs walls, when it leaves... it leaves a trail. What is it?

80 - What is it that the more you have, the less afraid you are?

81 - I run along the entire yard but always remain still... who am I?

82 - When you buy it, it's black; when you use it, it's red; when it ends, it's white. What is it?

83 - When it leaks, it's a problem; when it doesn't leak, it's a success. What are we referring to?

84 - If it drops, you won't hear it anymore. What is it?

85 - What is it that burns when you put it in your mouth but doesn't if you hold it in your hand?

86 - It's as light as air, has many colors, but if you touch it... it bursts. What is it?

87 - What enters first and then opens the door?

88 - It has existed for millions of years, but every month it is new... it can be full but never overflows. What is it?

89 - Its teeth pass between your teeth. What is it?

90 - It can fly from hand to hand if it escapes far away; with a thread, it flies nearby; it's not an airplane or a bird. What is it?

91 - What cries without having eyes and flies without having wings?

92 - Who is it that goes under a car every day but never gets hurt?

93 - Despite being close, they can never see each other. Who are they?

94 - What is it that the more capable it is, the more it receives trash?

95 - Who is it that can't wait to remove the problem?

96 - I have my head out and my body inside, but I disappear entirely if you scare me. Who am I?

Intermediate Riddle Solutions

1 – A sponge

2 – A towel

3 – A problem

4 – A bottle

5 – A table

6 – A candy

7 – An egg

8 – A dictionary

9 – A candle

10 – A match

11 – A horse and its rider

12 – A postage stamp

13 – A diary

14 – A battery

15 – A river

16 – Shadow

17 – One is bald

18 – A glove

19 – A needle / A potato

20 – Second place

21 – Hailstones

22 – A mirror

23 – A cloud

24 – Fire

25 – A volcano

26 – Salami

27 – A crane

28 – Earth

29 – A blackboard

30 – A priest

31 – The letter "D"

32 – A refrigerator

33 – An egg

34 – The plate

35 – The stars

36 – An envelope

37 – A surfboard

38 – Shadow

39 – The eyes

40 – A cold

41 – Sleep

42 – The doctor

43 – A notebook

44 – Pasta

45 – A compass

46 – A priest

47 – A butcher

48 – Holidays

49 – A path

50 – Teeth

51 – A screw

52 – The bed

53 – A die

54 – A rubber band

55 – A coin

56 – The wind

57 – The chessboard

58 – The firefly

59 – The cricket

60 – Holidays

61 – The hand

62 – The comb

63 – The dictionary

64 – The sponge

65 – The feet

66 – Money

67 – A pocket

68 – The cicada

69 – Tears

70 – Rice

71 – An elevator

72 – The net

73 – The tomato

74 – A path

75 – Fork

76 – The sun

77 – The hours

78 – The flag

79 – The snail

80 – Courage

81 – The fence

82 – Charcoal

83 – At the faucet

84 – A call

85 – Chili pepper

86 – Soap bubble

87 – The key

88 – The moon

89 – The fork

90 – A kite

91 – The cloud

92 – A mechanic

93 – Eyes

94 – The bin

95 – A doctor

96 – A snail

MASTER RIDDLES
(1-95)

1 - The more you make, the more you leave behind. What are they?

2 - If I have it, I don't share it. If I share it, I don't have it. What is it?

3 - They come out at night without being called, and disappear during the day without being stolen. What are they?

4 - It's light as a feather but no one, no matter how strong, can hold it for very long.

5 - What is yours but used by others more often than you?

6 - It needs an answer, but doesn't ask a question. What is it?

7 - I have a large piggy bank, 25 cm long and 15 cm wide. How many coins can I fit into an empty piggy bank?

8 - If four people can repair four bicycles in four hours, how many bicycles can eight people repair in eight hours?

9 - The person who made it didn't want it. The person who bought it didn't need it. The person who used it didn't see it. What is it?

10 - What is something you will never see again?

11 – What is the center of gravity?

12 – What is put on a table, and cut...but never eaten?

13 – I am a word. If you pronounce me wrong, I am right. If you pronounce me right, I am wrong. What word am I?

14 – I will come, but I won't arrive today. What am I?

15 – It's not seawater, not from a spring, not collected from the ground, but on your forehead.

16 – You can only keep it by giving it away to someone else.

17 – It loses its head in the morning, then gets it back in the evening. What is it?

18 – What can you serve...but not eat?

19 – If it ends up in the net...it made a mistake in passing. What is it?

20 – It has a head. Feet. Four legs. What is it?

21 - What can you hold without touching it?

22 - What can you make that you can't see?

23 - What can never ever be put into a pot?

24 - Inside a car there are two fathers and two sons, but only three people. How is this possible?

25 - Which three positive numbers give the same result when added together, or when multiplied together?

26 - Imagine a bookshelf with several books. One book is the fourth counting from the left, and the sixth counting from the right. How many books are on the bookshelf in total?

27 - If you ask a girl her age and she responds, "In two years I will be twice the age I was five years ago," how old is she?

28 - Everyone needs it, but its usually given without acceptance. What is it?

29 - My life can end in a few hours, what I produce slowly devours me. If thin, I am fast, if fat, I am slow. But the wind is what scares me. What am I?

30 - You bury it when it's born and dig it up when it's dead. What are we talking about?

31 – I leave everyone amazed when I work. Who am I?

32 – They buy me dirty with dirt, they pass me on to others when I'm boiling. What am I?

33 – I stay at home on beautiful days, I only go out on ugly ones. What am I?

34 – I'm interested in the past, I'm created in the present, and the future can never change me. Who/what am I?

35 – What is extracted from water but disappears in water?

36 – You throw it away when you need to use it, you pick it up when you don't need it anymore. What is it?

37 – When it's not there, we hope it doesn't come, but when it's there, we don't want to lose it. What is it?

38 – I have many rings, but I've never been married. What am I?

39 – We didn't exist before you were here, but now we are everywhere. What are we talking about?

40 – I'm a half small circle but no sea can ever fill me. What really fills me, then fills you too. What am I?

41 – This is how all endings begin.

42 – I join two people but I join them into one.

43 – Everyone likes me, some take me and some give me. I've had many masters, I go around here and there. What am I?

44 – What goes into water and doesn't get wet, through thorns and doesn't get pricked, enters the house and doesn't stay?

45 - What begins, but has no end, and is instead the end of what begins?

46 - What is that question, to which one can never honestly answer yes?

47 - It can run, but not walk. It has a mouth, but cannot talk. It has a bed, but never sleeps. What is it?

48 - It has cities, but no houses. It has rivers, but no fish. It has forests, but no trees. What is it?

49 - It has no hands, no feet, no arms, no wings... yet it can climb to the ceiling. What is it?

50 - It has invisible roots, higher than trees it stands, up among the clouds it goes, yet it will never grow. What are we talking about?

51 - It has no voice, yet it makes a cry. It has no wings, yet it can fly. It has no teeth, yet it bites. It has no mouth, yet it sings. What is it?

52 - Without lid, key, or hinge, a chest contains a golden sphere. What is it?

53 - What lives without breathing, seems cold as death, drinks but is never thirsty, and makes no sound?

54 - We're eight and always go forth, never back, to save our rulers from danger and attack. Who are we?

55 - If you look at the numbers on my face, you will see that there is no trace of 13. Who am I?

56 - If you say my name, I no longer exist. Who am I?

57 - What has flesh and bloodless veins, and a heart of stone?

58 - In the pit of boiling waters, sticks go in and snakes come out. What are we talking about?

59 - We have legs but no feet, you use us for walking but also for sleeping. Who are we?

60 - What can be big or small, but in the dark it leads you by the hand?

61 – It has six faces, but not for reflecting. It has twenty-one eyes, but can't see. What is it?

62 – No one wants me on them, and advertisements say "stay away". I keep the body cool when the temperature threatens, but when I'm "cold" I bathe the forehead and face. What am I?

63 – Originally from the tropics, but not from gardens, its roasted and ground seeds are the most tasty for adults and children. What are we talking about?

64 – You can't see it, but it increases and decreases…usually a glass of water is enough to turn it off. What is it?

65 – It can be made of sand or defended by soldiers, but also of stacked papers or tarot cards. What is it?

66 – We are industrious and numerous, we move in columns like in war, and we live underground. Who are we?

67 – It's so delicate that a breath or a word can break it. What is it?

68 – There's a canvas that no painter can paint. What is it?

69 – It's white: when it's there, you can't see, when it's not there, you can. What is it?

70 – We are five and always close, so much that when we dress we wear only one clothing item. What are we?

71 – The more you drag it, the shorter it gets. What is it?

72 – Water, tea, wine don't quench me, but I can't go without drinking. What am I?

73 – It sells products that are always fresh but that no one eats...who is it?

74 – What falls from a skyscraper and doesn't get hurt, but gets ruined if it falls in the water?

75 – Who jumps in and doesn't get wet? Assuming it's not raining.

76 – It can be long or short, has white and black keys that can be played as you like but the strings, no, those can't be seen.

77 – It comes from the tree and is very thin, useful to adults and children, you can stack as many as you want, it's white, clean and it's not a leaf. What is it?

78 – What is lower with a head and taller without a head?

79 – What can be stretched but not shortened, and in the end returns to its original state?

80 – What is not a prize, but can be won by playing?

81 – It's a net but not for fishing, it is not a boat but used for surfing. What is it?

82 – When it moves it jumps, if it can, it lives in the water but it's not a fish. Who have we described?

83 – Who is not a king, but wears a crown, and wakes up at dawn and doesn't forgive?

84 – It's immense and holds up large objects, even like buildings, but it can't hold up a pebble. What is it?

85 - If your eyes are open, you can't find it, but if you find it, you close them immediately. What is it?

86 - No one can see it, no one can touch it, it's very fast but can be heard, and it can be loud or gentle. What is it?

87 - In the morning you leave it behind, in the evening you find it again, and you sleep with it. What is it?

88 - You wear it for the first time and it hurts, but from the second time, it doesn't. What is it?

89 - What is something that, if it's big in your pocket, then the pocket is empty?

90 - It's an object with two parts, and when they come together, they divide. What object is it?

91 - There are many of them, and even if you can't see them, you must observe them all, or else you'll be in trouble. What are they?

92 - What is something that can only grow as long as there's life?

93 - You can see it from far away, but if you try to get closer to see it better, it moves away. What is it?

94 - What is something that appears when you close your hand and then disappears when you open it?

95 - They're always on your hands, and even though you leave them everywhere, you always carry them with you. What are we talking about?

Master riddle solutions

1 - Footsteps

2 - A secret

3 - The stars

4 - Breath

5 - Your name

6 - The telephone

7 - One (after that, it's not empty anymore)

8 - Sixteen

9 - A coffin

10 - Yesterday

11 - The letter "v"

12 - A deck of cards

13 - "Wrong"

14 - Tomorrow

15 - Sweat

16 - Your word

17 - The pillow

18 - A tennis ball

19 - The trapeze artist

20 - A bed

21 - The conversation

22 - Noise

23 - Its lid

24 - I am a grandfather, and his son, who is the father of his grandson.

25 - 1,2,3.

26 - Nine

27 - Twelve

28 - Advice

29 - A candle

30 - A plant

31 - The dentist

32 - A potato

33 - An umbrella

34 - A story

35 - Salt

36 - An anchor

37 - War

38 - A chain

39 - Fingerprints

40 - A colander

41 - With the letter "E"

42 - A wedding ring

43 - Money

44 - The sun

45 - Death

46 - Are you sleeping?

47 - A river

48 - A map

49 - Smoke

50 - A mountain

51 - Wind

52 - An egg

53 - Fish

54 - Chess pawns

55 - A clock

56 - Silence

57 - Olives

58 - Spaghetti

59 - Pants

60 - A shadow

61 - Dice

62 - Sweat

63 - The cocoa tree

64 - Thirst

65 - Castle

66 - Ants

67 - Silence

68 - A spider's web

69 - Fog

70 - Fingers

71 - A cigarette

72 - A car

73 - A florist

74 - Paper

75 - A soccer goalkeeper

76 - A piano

77 - A sheet of paper

78 - A pillow

79 - An elastic band

80 - Boredom

81 - The internet

82 - A frog

83 - A rooster

84 - The sea

85 - Sleep

86 – Sound

87 - Sound

88 - An earring

89 - Space

90 - Scissors

91 - Laws

92 - Age

93 - The horizon

94 - A fist

95 - Fingerprints

THE CHARM OF QUIZZES

The etymology of the term "quiz" is uncertain. However, everyone agrees on one thing. The expression is not originally related to any activity that has something in common with games structured on "question and answer". In fact, this term refers to a series of questions designed to test an individual's memory, preparation, culture, or sagacity (intuition). In American English, it indicates an extravagant and eccentric person. Only since 1807 has it been used in the sense that we attribute to it, and there are multiple versions, even legendary ones, of how this strange term entered the common vocabulary.

An unconfirmed theory is that it goes back to antiquity, from the Latin "quis" (who?) and then from there to "quiz". Or as an abbreviation of the English "inquisition", according to a typical tendency of this language. But all this remains in the realm of suggestive hypotheses, and the most improbable of these risks being a real "urban legend": an Irish theater impresario from Dublin, would have had to insert, for a bet, a meaningless term ("quiz") into the speech of his city. He would have written it on all the walls within his reach with red paint, and the next day people would have started talking about it and repeating it, wondering what it meant and why it was everywhere, implicitly associating it with the meaning of "puzzle", "question".

As mentioned, what interests us is the current meaning, and a single quiz is nothing more than a question, and quizzes are a series of questions, designed to test one's preparation but also to play and have fun, competing and measuring one's memory and knowledge. Quizzes can contain questions of all kinds, from school subjects to basic general knowledge, to more specific but still easily approachable topics, such as sports, cinema, and cartoons. As with riddles, it's not good for them to be too "sectarian" because never knowing the answer isn't fun, but it's equally inadvisable for them to be too easy: always answering correctly without effort or "risk" is boring.

It's clear that even not knowing the answer and evaluating the solutions can be useful in terms of learning, acquiring knowledge, and personal growth. Playing with quizzes alone or in a group has always been a popular pastime. If you're in a group, among peers or in a family, you can challenge each other, and then competition makes everything even more fun. It's no coincidence that themed board games have been very successful, not to mention online games or recent apps.

Challenging oneself or others, starting from one's personal preparation, like the great contestants of the most celebrated television quizzes, is a "great classic" of entertainment and pastime for adults and, especially, for young people and children.

GENERAL KNOWLEDGE QUIZZES

1 - What is the largest mammal in the world?

2 - How many legs do spiders have?

3 - What is the largest continent of all?

4 - How many continents are there in total?

5 - What is the marine animal with eight legs?

6 - Which planet has rings?

7 - How many and which colors are in the rainbow?

8 - What food do whales eat? And what does it consist of?

9 - What is both a vegetable and a fruit?

10 - Which animal represents the zodiac sign Cancer?

11 - What is the fastest land animal of all?

12 - It is found in Africa, and its colossal trunk makes it instantly recognizable. It is the...

13 - Why were Native Americans given this name?

14 - Mount Everest, with its 8,848 meters, is the highest peak on Earth, and is located in the Asian continent, in the Himalayas. On the border of which states?

15 - Which animal, passionate about plumbing, builds dams?

16 - What is the largest desert on Earth?

17 - What is the name of the Tuscan city famous for the Leaning Tower?

18 - Even if you throw it as far as possible, it will always come back. What is this object called?

19 - How many digits does a dog have on its front paws?

20 - One of the most famous flags is the Stars and Stripes. Which country does it represent? And how many stripes are there? And how many stars?

21 - Monferrato is an area known mainly for vineyards and wine products. In which Italian region is it located?

22 - What is the name of the ancient constructions, still visible today, that were erected in Egypt as burial monuments?

23 - La Fenice Theater is famous worldwide. In which Italian city is it located?

24 - The spleen is a lymphatic system organ about the size of a fist, covered externally by fibrous tissue. In which part of the human body is it located?

25 - Whistles and buzzing, itching: these are the typical symptoms of otitis. They may be associated with fever, chills, nausea, vomiting, and diarrhea. Which human body organ does it affect?

26 - Miguel Cervantes Saavedra, a Spaniard from Madrid, was a writer, poet, and playwright. What is his most famous novel?

27 - In Greek mythology, Apollo was the god of the sun, arts, music, and medicine. Who was his father?

28 - What is, in alphabetical order, the first month of the year?

29 - Which animal is affected by the dangerous disease distemper?

30 - In a famous poem by Giosuè Carducci, it reads, "under the mistral, the sea howls and turns white." What is the mistral?

31 - Wall Street is the most important American stock exchange, located on the street of the same name, in the Manhattan district, in the city of...?

32 - In which northern Italian city is Sforza Castle located?

33 - Which monster, according to Greek mythology, was imprisoned by Minos in the labyrinth?

34 - Which 19th-century Italian novel features the timid priest Don Abbondio as a character?

35 - What profession does a worker generally have if they periodically use a billhook?

36 - What is the name of the iron structure erected in Paris for the 1889 World Exposition?

37 - What is the name of the sea that separates the Italian coast from the Albanian coast?

38 - How many men did Giuseppe Garibaldi have with him when he landed in Sicily in 1860?

39 - In which Italian province can you find the sea, the baths, the promenade, and the attractions of Versilia?

40 - Which Italian poet wrote the lyric "The Solitary Sparrow"?

41 - Everyone knows what ketchup is. But what is the etymology of this English term? And what did it originally mean?

42 - A zoologist generally studies animals. What is the name of the scholar who primarily devotes themselves to insects?

43 - What is someone afraid of when they declare their arachnophobia?

44 - Parthenope was, in ancient Greek mythology, a siren. Which Italian city was formerly called that, so much so that its inhabitants are still called "Parthenopeans"?

45 - The first day of each month in the Roman calendar, that of the new moon when it followed the lunar cycle.

46 - Mikado, as well as the name of tasty chocolate biscuits, was also the nickname by which the emperors of which country were formerly called?

47 - What is the name of the science that studies and classifies coins from a historical and artistic point of view?

48 - Of which animal breed is a dog lover passionate and in love with?

49 - What was the title attributed to the Head of State in the ancient Republic of Venice?

50 - The acronym is a name formed by using the initials of multiple words. So what does FIAT mean?

General knowledge quiz solutions

1 - The blue whale

2 - Eight

3 - Asia

4 - Six

5 - Octopus

6 - Saturn

7 - Seven: Violet, Indigo, Blue, Green, Yellow, Orange, Red.

8 - Plankton, floating aquatic organisms.

9 - Tomato

10 - A crab

11 - The cheetah

12 - Baobab

13 - They dyed their skin red and wore fox skin

14 - China and Nepal

15 - The beaver

16 - The Sahara Desert.

17 - Pisa

18 - Boomerang

19 - 5

20 - The American flag, 13 stripes and 50 stars

21 - Piedmont

22 - The pyramids

23 - Venice

24 - Abdomen

25 - The ear

26 - Don Quixote

27 - Jupiter

28 - August

29 - Dog

30 - A wind

31 - New York

32 - Milan

33 - Minotaur

34 - The Betrothed

35 - Farmer

36 - The Eiffel Tower

37 - Adriatic

38 - One thousand

39 - Lucca

40 - Leopardi

41 - The term has a Chinese origin, koe-chiap, and means "fermented fish sauce."

42 - Entomologist

43 - Afraid of spiders

44 - Naples

45 - Calends

46 - Japan

47 - Numismatics

48 - Dogs

49 - Doge

50 - Fabbrica Italiana Automobili Torino

FILM & CARTOON QUIZZES

51 - Mickey Mouse, Donald Duck, Dumbo, The 101 Dalmatians... who is the most famous cartoon creator in the world?

52 - According to the legend of the Knights of the Round Table, what is the name of the magical sword that King Arthur uses to conquer the kingdom (after pulling it from a rock)?

53 - Harry Potter, the protagonist of the famous saga, receives a curious gift from Rubeus Hagrid when he turns 11. A snow owl. What is its name...?

54 - In the famous Snow White fairy tale, the Seven Dwarfs are the protagonists. What are their names?

55 - Various directors of Batman movies have made it suitably dark and spooky. Which city are we talking about?

56 - In which country was Charlie Chaplin (1889-1977) born, one of the most important and influential actors and filmmakers of the 20th century?

57 - The main characters of the "Mickey Mouse" comic strip are all anthropomorphic animals. What kind of animal is Goofy, Mickey's friend?

58 - Son of Zeus and Hera, half deity and half man, in the famous Disney film, he wants to prove he's a true hero to earn a place on Mount Olympus. Who is he?

59 - It's the "crazy" beetle in an old Disney film. What is its name?

60 - "Harry Potter and the Goblet of Fire" is a film adaptation of the eponymous book by J.K. Rowling, which is the ... book in the saga.

61 - In a famous 90's film, they were "fried green tomatoes at the Whistle Stop Cafe". What were they?

62 - Hakuna Matata is the signature song of a hugely successful animated film. Which one?

63 - "IT", Stephen King's bestseller, which has recently been adapted into yet another successful film, features a clown. What is his name?

64 - The Disney film "The Little Mermaid" features a mermaid princess, curious about the human world and not fully satisfied with her life under the sea, in the kingdom of Atlantica. What is her name?

65 - In the same film, the antagonist is a wicked sea witch, the octopus woman called...

66 - Director James Cameron won eleven Oscars for his historical and dramatic blockbuster starring Leonardo DiCaprio and Kate Winslet, as Jack and Rose. Which one?

67 - In the popular American cartoon "The Simpsons", the young people of Springfield are fans of another "cartoon" featuring a cat and a mouse. What are their names?

68 - What is the name of the underwater city in the Pacific Ocean where the successful SpongeBob SquarePants cartoon series is set?

69 - Brandon Lee, the unfortunate actor made famous by the film "The Crow" (released posthumously), was the son of a true action cinema icon. Who are we talking about?

70 - Which famous actor and dancer was made even more famous by the character he played in Quentin Tarantino's masterpiece, "Pulp Fiction"?

71 - What is the name of the fictional Sicilian village where Tornatore's film "Cinema Paradiso" is set?

72 - How many films are in the Harry Potter saga?

73 - "One Ring to rule them all, One Ring to find them, One Ring to bring them all and in the darkness bind them", which film trilogy does this rhyme refer to?

74 - What is the name of the lead actress who stars alongside Richard Gere in the popular film "Pretty Woman"?

75 - Asia Argento is the daughter of a great Italian film director...

76 - What material is Cinderella's lost slip

77 - The Big Bad Wolf from the Three Little Pigs, dating back to the 1930s, also has a name besides the "Bad" epithet. What is this name?

78 - The Italian-American boxer made famous on the big screen by Sylvester Stallone's portrayal.

79 - The little green man who wanted to phone home in the famous 1982 film by Steven Spielberg.

80 - Where did the characters Marty McFly and DOC want or have to return to in a famous 1980s film?

81 - How many bandits threaten the peace of little Kevin in the movie "Home Alone"?

82 - The sequel to the cartoon Pocahontas is called "Journey to the New World." To which "new world" does the title refer? What major European city does the girl visit?

83 - Which American actor brought the famous movie character Forrest Gump to life?

84 - Where does Checco Zalone fall from in the title of one of his hilarious films?

85 - What type of "pasta" is paired with the term western to indicate a specific film genre?

86 - With whom does Kevin Costner dance in his most famous western-themed film?

87 - Leonardo DiCaprio is a fur trapper. Believed dead by his companions, he is abandoned; he does not die and carries out his revenge. What is the name of this film?

88 - Oscar-winning film by Roberto Benigni, about the horror of concentration camps and the Jewish Holocaust. What title are we talking about?

89 - An Italian actor, and Emilian, among the most famous of the new generation, launched by Ligabue in "Radiofreccia" and now starring in many films and TV series (like "1992"). Who is he?

90 - In which series of Gomorrah is the character Ciro Di Marzio, "The Immortal," killed?

91 - Around the exploits of which famous criminal organization does the TV series "Romanzo Criminale" revolve?

92 - Which famous film and TV actor plays the lead role in the award-winning saga "The Truth About the Harry Quebert Affair"?

93 - What are the "101" in the famous Disney film?

94 - In which city is "The Great Beauty," the last Italian film to win an Oscar, set?

95 - Which actor has been an ideal sidekick for the great Christian De Sica, in many Christmas "cinepanettoni"?

96 - "A Star is Born" is a film starring Bradley Cooper and a very famous American pop singer-songwriter. Who are we referring to?

97 - What is the name of the strongest soccer player of all time, acting for once in the epic movie "Victory"?

98 - Who returns in one of the episodes of "The Lord of the Rings" trilogy?

FILM & CARTOON QUIZ SOLUTIONS

51 - Walt Disney

52 - Excalibur

53 - Hedwig

54 - Doc, Grumpy, Sleepy, Bashful, Happy, Dopey, Sneezy.

55 - Gotham City

56 - England

57 - A dog

58 - Hercules

59 - Herbie

60 - Fourth

61 - Tomatoes

62 - The Lion King

63 - Pennywise

64 - Ariel

65 - Ursula

66 - Titanic

67 - Itchy and Scratchy

68 - Bikini Bottom

69 - Bruce Lee

70 - John Travolta

71 - Giancaldo

72 - Eight

73 - The Lord of the Rings

74 - Julia Roberts

75 - Dario Argento

76 - Crystal

77 - Zeke

78 - Rocky

79 - ET

80 - (Back) to the Future.

81 - Two

82 - London, England

83 - Tom Hanks

84 - From the Clouds

85 - Spaghetti

86 - With Wolves

87 - Revenant

88 - Life is Beautiful

89 - Stefano Accorsi

90 - The third

91 - The Magliana Gang

92 - Patrick Dempsey

93 - Dalmatians

94 - Rome

95 - Massimo Boldi

96 - Lady Gaga

97 - Pelé

98 - The king

VARIOUS SPORTS QUIZZES

101 - In soccer, the penalty kick is also called by the .... considering the distance from the goal line.

102 - One of the most famous "faults" in volleyball is whistled during the serve when the ball is not hit simultaneously by both hands and therefore takes a rotation. What is it called?

103 - The All Blacks, in rugby, are the most famous national team in the world. But not everyone can associate the battle name with the real name of the country they represent.

104 - Diego Armando Maradona, who recently passed away, played not only for Napoli but also for a strong Spanish team.

105 - They were nicknamed the "Coca Cola" Olympic Games, from the main sponsor of the event. Which edition are we talking about?

106 - The acronym is a name formed using the initials of several words. What does CONI mean?

107 - There are 4 bases in baseball and they are essential for the game. They are arranged to form a square (diamond) within which the pitching mound is located. What are they called, in order?

108 - What is the name, in baseball, for the batter's elimination?

109 - Track and field is the queen of the Olympics. How many different events take place during a Games edition that can be traced back to it?

110 - Which Italian soccer team won the first championship in 1898?

111 - What is the nickname of Gazzetta dello Sport, the most famous sports newspaper in Italy?

112 - The old Champions Cup for throwing has changed its name, for some decades, adopting an English name. Which one?

113 - How many fouls must be whistled in basketball for the same player to be expelled in FIBA?

114 - Boxing categories are determined by weight, which each individual boxer must conform to. How much do you have to weigh to compete in the "super heavyweight" category?

115 - How many players are there in a "classic" rugby field? Meaning, for each individual team.

116 - What is the name of the Argentine volleyball coach who led the Italian national team to become the strongest in the world?

117 - How long does a rugby match last, in terms of minutes?

118 - What is the nickname of the United States basketball team whenever they participate in an Olympics or World Cup?

119 - What is the nickname of the Italian water polo national team?

120 - Swimming is divided into four different specialties, depending on the style adopted to advance in the water. What are these "styles"?

121 - How many periods is an American football game divided into?

122 - The acronym is a name formed using the initials of several words. What does NBA mean?

123 - What are the specialties of a triathlon, the individual multidisciplinary sport? And in what order should they be tackled?

124 - How many meters away from the net can we find, in a volleyball court, the drawn line that divides the first from the second line?

125 - In which European country does the famous stage cycling race called "Vuelta" take place?

126 - What is the name of the men's cycling race, in line and on the road, that starts from Lombardy and arrives in Liguria?

127 - What are the team colors of the Borussia Dortmund soccer team?

128 - Every year the Italian national rugby team participates in the Six Nations Tournament. What are the other five nations automatically enrolled?

129 - Which Grand Prix of the official Formula One circuit is commonly called "of Italy"?

130 - What is one of the most famous fouls that can be whistled in basketball? Related to an error in judgment in the mode of moving with the ball in hand.

131 - What is the name of the track and field specialty, both men's and women's, where the athlete must compete in ten different disciplines?

132 - How many athletes from a team can be on the field at the same time, in volleyball?

133 - The square structure, delimited by ropes, inside which a boxing match takes place, is called...

134 - What is the name of the lane in the pool where you swim?

135 - In soccer, during a dangerous free kick, the goalkeeper sets up some teammates to form a wall between himself and the ball. That construction is called...

136 - What is the name of the sports facility designed to host cycling competitions, particularly track cycling races?

137 - What is the name of the soccer stadium where Roma and Lazio play?

138 - In cycling, multi-day races are called...

139 - Men's and women's race over a distance of 42 km and 195 meters. The most famous is the New York one. What is it called?

140 - It is awarded to the team that comes first in the Italian soccer championship. What are we talking about?

141 - There are different types of tennis courts, regarding the playing surface. The main variants are three. Which ones?

142 - The aim of the game is to hole a ball by hitting it with different types of clubs, following the sequence of holes on a course. It is an outdoor sport, considered very relaxing. Which one?

143 - It's the soccer team of Bergamo...

144 - How long is an outdoor track and field track (referring to the first lane)?

145 - With discus and hammer, it's the third most famous throw among track and field specialties. What are we referring to?

146 - In volleyball matches, they enter and leave the field unlimitedly, wearing a different jersey from the rest of the team. What role is it?

147 - What is it called, in rugby, the moment when players from both teams face each other trying to gain yards against each other?

148 - Where do the Italian Tennis Open take place?

149 - What is the name of volleyball played on a sand court?

150 - It is worn, at the Giro d'Italia cycling race, by the leader in the overall standings. What are we talking about?

Various sports quiz solutions

101 - Eleven meters

102 - Double touch

103 - New Zealand

104 - Barcelona

105 - Atlanta 1996

106 - Italian National Olympic Committee

107 - Home Base, First Base, Second Base, Third Base

108 - Strike

109 - Twenty-seven

110 - Genoa FC

111 - La rosea

112 - Champions League

113 - Five

114 - More than 91 kg

115 - Fifteen

116 - Julio Velasco

117 - Eighty minutes

118 - Dream Team

119 - Settebello

120 - Freestyle, backstroke, breaststroke, butterfly.

121 - Four

122 - National Basketball Association

123 - Swimming, cycling, running

124 - Three

125 - Spain

126 - Milan-San Remo

127 - Yellow and black

128 - England, France, Ireland, Wales, Scotland.

129 - Monza

130 - "Traveling"

131 - Decathlon

132 - Six

133 - Ring

134 - Lane

135 - Wall

136 - Velodrome

137 - Olimpico

138 - Stage races

139 - Marathon

140 - Scudetto

141 - Grass, Clay, Hardcourt.

142 - Golf

143 - Atalanta

144 - 400 meters

145 - Javelin

146 - Libero

147 - Scrum

148 - Rome

149 - Beach Volleyball

150 - Pink jersey

CONCLUSIONS

DEEP DIVE: CHILDREN AND LATERAL THINKING

Lateral thinking, often mentioned in the titles of riddle, quiz, and charade books, is intuitive in nature and therefore serves as a genuine alternative to so-called "vertical" thinking, the type of logical and consequential reasoning that sometimes makes us "trapped" and limited in our way of seeing, interpreting, and consequently interacting with the reality that surrounds us. As time goes by, our beliefs become more and more rooted, firm, and settled. Moreover, in the hyper-technological and connected world, they risk following others' patterns: we rely on the opinions we read, and we are unable to think independently.

Vertical thinking, or consequential logical thinking, is still useful, but it achieves its effectiveness when combined with lateral thinking, which can expand beyond its limits and boundaries, seeking further solutions outside of it. Vertical thinking helps us solve a problem directly by relying on experience and acquired skills. Lateral thinking, on the other hand, makes different use of available information.

Logical thinking does not always lead to a solution, though; sometimes it can get stuck, jam, and when it goes back, it tends to retrace the same steps, those of past information and experiences, thus forming increasingly rigid and schematic "neuronal grooves". At this point, the temptation to give up is strong, and we tell ourselves, "it's impossible to find a solution!"

There is a whole series of games designed specifically to develop lateral thinking. We mention them because our text contains many riddles related to this concept but not "specifically designed for" it. Children and young people should gradually approach lateral thinking, embracing the culture of "problem solving", and then train to develop the full potential of this method, also through the use of riddles and exercises at a higher level. For example, like this one:

Imagine you find yourself in a room with only two doors. Going through the first one, you will be instantly pulverized by a gigantic lens capable of concentrating sunlight. Opening the second one, you will be hit by the flames of a powerful dragon. Which of the two doors do you choose?

Solution: the first one. Just wait for nightfall. It's always better than waiting for the dragon's death.

Lateral thinking, identified in 1967 by Maltese psychologist Edward De Bono, is increasingly important because, in a society set to be increasingly dominated by "machines", it will be an identifying characteristic of the human race. Computers, in fact, can think only logically and sequentially. Not laterally. In the example above, they would not know the answer. They cannot think "outside the box"; they lack the intuition and creativity that we must instead seek to promote in children and young people.

Some examples of puzzles of this type can be the starting point for a great discussion between parents and children:

A man lives in a penthouse of a New York skyscraper. Every morning he takes the elevator down to the ground floor and leaves the building. Upon his return, however, the elevator takes him only halfway up the skyscraper, and he has to walk up the rest of the floors (unless it is raining outside). How can this be explained?

Solution: The man is a dwarf and cannot reach the top floor button unless it is raining outside, in which case he can press the button of his floor with an umbrella.

A man and his son are involved in a serious car accident. Unfortunately, the man dies on the spot, and when the rescuers arrive, the boy is in critical condition. The ambulance immediately takes him to the hospital for a delicate surgical operation. However, when the surgeon sees the boy, he immediately says, "I cannot perform the operation; this is my son!"

Solution: The surgeon is the mother.

A black man, a bit drunk, dressed in black and wearing a black mask, is staggering in the middle of a road with black asphalt, right behind a curve. The road is deserted, the streetlights are off, and there are no moon or stars in the sky, obscured by black clouds. The houses overlooking the street are all painted black, with closed windows and the lights off.

Suddenly, from behind the curve, a black car with its headlights off and speeding appears. Yet, the driver manages, without difficulty and with a swift turn, to avoid the black man. How can this event be explained?

Solution: The driver - the one in the black car with the headlights off - has no difficulty seeing the black man in the middle of the black road simply because the story takes place during the day.

DEEP DIVE: HUMOROUS RIDDLES

This text does not include riddles whose main objective is not to stimulate a correct answer or reasoning, but rather to make people laugh. Technically, they are more related to joke books or other games like "colmi," which we mention later. However, "funny" riddles are very popular among children, the best way to exercise the mind without even realizing it. And once again, they are a way to spend time together with friends and family, enjoying leisure time. Of course, the right solution must be indicated in the shortest possible time. Here below, as a postface and "bonus track," we provide 25 of the funniest examples, complete with solutions.

1 - What is the hitchhiker's favorite fairy tale?

2 - What does a tomato do in the morning?

3 - Where does the exception to the rule live?

4 - What does a rooster do in the water?

5 - What does a bubble bath exclaim while running away?

6 - How do you kill a watchmaker?

7 - What is the name of Alibaba's son?

8 - Why is the sea salty?

9 - What did the circle say to the triangle?

10 - What did the Last of the Mohicans say?

11 - Why is the snake brave?

12 - What does the doorbell do at the monkey's house?

13 - Why do tomatoes never sleep?

14 - Why did Moses stop in front of the Red Sea?

15 - Why is the book always warm?

16 - What does a coffee bean do on the train?

17 - What does a cook do when bored?

18 - What do potatoes say when they are in danger?

19 - Why are math books sad?

20 - What does a little bird do inside a computer?

Solutions

1 - Thumbelina

2 - Salsa

3 - In an exceptional street

4 - Floats

5 - I have no shampoo

6 - With the pendulum

7 - Alibaby

8 - Because there are anchovies

9 - Something doesn't square up

10 - Wait for me

11 - Because it has cold blood

12 - King Kong

13 - Because of the Russian salad

14 - He was waiting for it to turn green

15 - Because it has a cover

16 - Espresso

17 - Stew

18 - We're fried

19 - Because they are full of problems

20 - Chip

DEEP DIVE: THE CHARADE

The charade is a puzzle game that consists of guessing a word through allusions and its decomposition into semantically autonomous elements. In other words, it is a very particular and very difficult type of riddle, even in terms of form. The charade is one of the most famous and enjoyable games involving words: often organized in verses - so that the rhyme comes to help - the charade consists of proposing to guess a word, which is discreetly and willingly alluded to in the title of the single game, through the combination of words that compose it. In a simple example (but don't think that the charade is a simple game), "baraonda" can be guessed by first identifying the words "bara" and "onda."

It is a refined game that exists in many variations and has its own jargon; and such was its grip on the collective imagination that it became the quintessential puzzle: in fact, in the figurative sense, the charade becomes the difficult problem to solve, the situation that is hard to figure out.

It is understood why it does not have citizenship in our text, as it is theoretically reserved for adults and... adults expert in puzzles or at least with some training behind them. We quickly propose an example for a more precise understanding. For those who become passionate about riddles and quizzes... charades can be a fun step forward.

My first remains after sawing the trunk,

with my second, Augustus argued,

my whole is unwrapped and has a sweet taste

Solution: The first word is CIOCCO, what remains after sawing the trunk, while the second is LATINO, the language used for arguing by Augustus. The whole, first + second, is CIOCCOLATINO, which indeed is unwrapped if you want to eat it and undoubtedly has a sweet taste.

IN CONCLUSION

Riddles and quizzes not only develop children's logical thinking and problem-solving skills, but they also help them to bet on themselves and their own potential. Equipping oneself with the courage to take a stand, communicate with others, accept "failure," and rejoice in success are essential components of growth and an exceptional educational tool. Research shows that the brain needs challenges to develop. Riddles and exercises are the best way to give the brain what it needs in terms of mental training. Long-term memory is another factor that children should practice from an early age, and not just children. In a world that encourages human relationships or knowledge exclusively through the web or social network connections, it is essential to cultivate strategies to allow young people to bond with their peers, compare themselves, and compete in inventiveness and creativity.

Play is a fundamental aspect of the growth of children and young people. It guarantees many physical and psychological benefits, crucial for their cognitive development. Reasoning, inventiveness, and memory are continually stimulated; it is the first channel through which young children can explore new things and assert their tastes, inclinations, and interests. It is essential to let them discover the flavor of ancient things, such as words: riddles, tongue twisters, rhymes, musicality, humor. And to lead them to be satisfied with the "things they know": material from school books or newspapers, magazines, or sports newspapers. Reading, watching, memorizing, cataloging. Knowing and understanding. Remembering.

The hope is that a text like this can represent a valid proposal and introduction to the world of quizzes and riddles of various kinds and levels, and spark interest in this world that only appears "vintage," but is more relevant than ever, if not essential.

Made in the USA
Columbia, SC
12 October 2023

24389625R00070